My Holiday in

Brazil

Jane Bingham

WAYLAND

Published in paperback in 2014 by Wayland
Copyright © Wayland 2014

Wayland
338 Euston Road
London NW1 3BH

Wayland Australia
Level 17/207 Kent Street
Sydney NSW 2000

Produced for Wayland by
White Thomson Publishing Ltd
www.wtpub.co.uk
+44 (0)843 2087 460

Senior Editor: Victoria Brooker
Editors: Jane Bingham/Steve White-Thomson
Designer: Ian Winton
Map artwork: Stefan Chabluk
Proofreader: Alice Harman

British Library Cataloguing in Publication Data
Bingham, Jane
   My holiday in Brazil
   1. Vacations – Brazil – Juvenile literature
   2. Brazil – Juvenile literature
   I. Title II. Brazil
   918.1'0466

   ISBN 978 07502 8302 1

Wayland is a division of Hachette Children's Books,
an Hachette UK company.
www.hachette.co.uk

Printed in China

10 9 8 7 6 5 4 3 2

Cover: Copacabana beach: Shutterstock/Catarina Belova;
Parrots: Dreamstime/F9photos.

p.1: Dreamstime/Renato Machado; p.5: Dreamstime/
Steve Allen; p.6: Shutterstock/Vitoriano Junior; p.7:
Shutterstock/Dr Morley Read; p.8: Shutterstock/Vinicius
Tupinamba; p.9 (top): Dreamstime/Alexandre Fagundes De
Fagundes; p.9 (bottom): Dreamstime/Alexandre Fagundes
De Fagundes; p.10: Dreamstime/Aguina; p.11 (top):
Dreamstime/Elder Salles; p.11 (bottom): Shutterstock/
gary yim; p.12: Dreamstime/Renato Machado; p.13:
Shutterstock/Catarina Belova; p.14: Shutterstock/Mark
Van Overmeire; p.15: Dreamstime/Celso Pupo rodrigues;
p.16: Dreamstime/Jeromaniac; p.17: Dreamstime/
Pixattitude; p.18: Dreamstime/Jorisvo; p.19 (top):
Shutterstock/Chris Pole; p.19 (middle): Shutterstock/
Eduardo Rivero; p.19 (bottom): Shutterstock/BMJ; p.20
(top): Shutterstock/Keith Sherwood; p.20 (bottom):
Dreamstime/F9photos; p.21: Shutterstock/guentermanaus;
p.22: Shutterstock/Alexandru Cristian Ciobanu; p.23:
Dreamstime/Alessio Moiola; p.24: Dreamstime/Carlos
Mora; p.25: Shutterstock/Luiz Rocha; p.26 (top):
Shutterstock/Celso Pupo; p.26 (bottom): Dreamstime/
Doogie360; p.27: Shutterstock/Rosa Maria Fiuza
Sciullo Faria; p.28: Shutterstock/Poznyakov; p.29 (top):
Dreamstime/David Alayo; p.29 (bottom): Dreamstime/
Henrique Araujo; p.30: Shutterstock/Piotr Krzeslak.

Contents

This is Brazil!

Brazil is a large country in the **continent** of South America. Most people travel there by aeroplane.

The Amazon rainforest covers most of northern Brazil.

Visitors usually fly to Rio de Janeiro to start their holiday.

This is a view of Rio from the air.

I saw mountains and beaches as our plane came into land. Brazil looked beautiful!

Speak Brazilian!

hello/hi
oi (oy)

yes
sim (sing)

no
não (now)

5

Sunshine and showers

It is usually hot and sunny in Brazil, especially in the north of the country.

The beaches on the north coast have sunshine all year round.

Things to take

- sun hat
- swimming costume
- sun cream

In the Amazon rainforest the weather is **tropical**. It feels hot and sticky and there are sudden rain storms.

Plants and trees grow strong and tall in the steamy heat of the rainforest.

We went for a walk in the rainforest. I got soaked, but the rain was warm!

Places to stay

Most visitors to Brazil stay in hotels. You can stay in a modern **skyscraper** or in a small country hotel. Some beautiful old buildings have been turned into hotels.

The city of Salvador on the east coast is a popular place to stay. It has many old buildings in the Portuguese style.

Portuguese style

People from Portugal began to **settle** in Brazil in the 1500s. They built houses and churches wherever they settled.

If you visit the Amazon rainforest, you will probably stay in a riverside hotel.

This hotel is in Manaus, on the banks of the Amazon River.

You may also stay in a rainforest lodge. Rainforest lodges are usually built of wood and are often raised above the ground on **stilts**.

Visitors have to cross a high bridge to reach this rainforest lodge!

Getting around

Many people travel around Brazil by plane. But some choose to go by coach so they can enjoy the countryside.

The best way to travel in cities is by bus. Most Brazilian cities have a very good bus service.

You can catch an electric trolley bus in São Paulo. The buses get their power from overhead cables.

Visitors can take some wonderful boat rides in Brazil.

Fast ferry boats cross the bay in Rio de Janeiro.

Tall riverboats glide slowly up the Amazon River. Some people stay on the boat for several days. At night they sleep in **hammocks**!

Wonderful Rio

A giant statue of Jesus stands on Mount Corcovado, looking down on Rio.

The city of Rio de Janeiro is often just called Rio. It lies between the mountains and the sea.

We took the **cog railway** to the top of Mount Corcovado. The views were amazing!

Rio has beautiful, sandy beaches. Its most famous beaches are Copacabana and Ipanema.

There are many hotels close to Copacabana beach.

Rio treats

Take a cable car – to the top of Sugarloaf Mountain

Learn about Brazil's native people – at the Museu do Índio

See parrots and monkeys – at the Jardim Zoológico

Cities and *favelas*

São Paulo and Rio are Brazil's largest cities, but neither of them is the capital. Brasília was built in the 1950s to be the capital city.

Brasília is famous for its unusual buildings.

City sights

modern skyscrapers – in São Paulo

busy food markets – in Recife

beautiful old buildings – in Salvador

When you visit Brazil's cities, you will see some people who are very poor. These people live in crowded areas, called *favelas*.

This *favela* is on a hill in Rio de Janeiro. It is just a few miles away from the smart hotels in the city centre.

Carnival time!

Brazilians really know how to enjoy themselves! At **carnival** time, they celebrate for four days and three nights. There are parades in the streets, with music and dancing.

People dress up in colourful costumes.

We went to the Rio carnival. It was the biggest party I've ever seen!

The largest carnival is held in Rio, but there are celebrations all over Brazil. Most towns and villages have their own festival.

The Bumba Meu Boi festival is very popular in northern Brazil. People act out a folk tale about a magic bull.

Wild wonders

Brazil has some astonishing natural sights. As well as the Amazon rainforest, you can see beautiful mountains, deserts, rivers and waterfalls.

Visitors can take a boat trip to see the Iguazu Falls.

Falls fact

The Iguazu Falls consist of 275 separate waterfalls in the shape of a giant horseshoe.

The Pantanal wetlands, in western Brazil, are home to some very unusual creatures.

Toucans use their giant bills to pick fruit from trees.

Caimans are a type of alligator.

Anteaters have long, narrow tongues to catch ants and other insects.

19

Exploring the Amazon

The best way to explore the Amazon rainforest is to take a trip up the Amazon River. You will see some fascinating sights on the river banks.

Some rainforest people live in wooden houses beside the river.

The parrots in the rainforest screeched really loudly. I had to cover my ears!

The Amazon Theatre was built in Manaus in the 1890s.

The Amazon River runs through two Brazilian cities. Belém is a busy port close to the river mouth. Manaus is 900 miles (1,450 km) down the river. It grew very rich in the 1890s, when rubber from the rainforest was sold at very high prices.

Be prepared!

You will need to protect yourself from insects on the river. Wear a long-sleeved top and trousers and use anti-insect cream.

People of Brazil

Brazilian people are very friendly, and they are really proud of their country!

These Brazilians are marching behind their country's flag.

Speak Brazilian!

how are you?
como vai? (com-o-**vye**)

what is your name?
como se chama?
(**com**-o-sey-**shum**-ah?)

my name is ...
meu nome é... (me-o-**nom**-ee-eh...)

Many Brazilians have Portuguese **ancestors**. The Brazilian language is a form of Portuguese.

These children belong to the Awá-Guajá people. Their ancestors have lived in the rainforest for thousands of years.

Some people live deep inside the Amazon rainforest. They hunt animals for food, and make food and medicines from plants and trees.

Losing homes

The people of the rainforest are in danger of losing their homes. They are being driven out of the forest by powerful companies that cut down the trees.

Eating Brazilian-style

Brazilians love to eat meat. There is also a great choice of fish, fruit and vegetables.

You will see some unusual fruit and vegetables for sale. Be prepared for some exciting new tastes!

Most Brazilian cities have large fishing ports. So there is plenty of fish to eat.

Moqueta (mo-keh-tah) is a very popular dish. It is a spicy stew made with fish or prawns.

On the menu

feijoada
(fey-zhoo-**ah**-dah) – a stew of meat and beans

vatapá
(vut-ah-**pah**) – a dish made with shrimps, coconut milk and bread

brigadeiros
(brig-ad-**eer**-us) – chocolate fudge sweets, eaten at children's parties

25

Shopping time

Brazilians have a great sense of style! You can buy fantastic clothes in a shopping centre or on a market stall.

Market stalls are good places to buy cheap clothes.

The money you spend in Brazil is called the real (hey-al).

If you want something hand-made, there is plenty of choice. You could buy a leather belt, a necklace made from seeds, or a carved wooden animal.

These wooden turtles and armadillos are based on real animals of Brazil.

Speak Brazilian!

how much does it cost?
quanto é? (kwan-too-**ey**)

please
por favor (por-fa-**vor**)

thank you
obrigado (ob-rig-**ah**-doh) (said by men and boys)
obrigada (ob-rig-**ah**-dah) (said by women and girls)

Fun and games

There are lots of active things to do in Brazil. You can go **snorkelling** in the sea. You can cycle along the coast around Rio. Or you can have fun in a water park.

It's great to cool off in a water park when it's really hot.

Other fun things to do:

Join in the dancing at a carnival.

Cheer on a beach volleyball team.

Watch a display of capoeira (cap-oo-weer-ra). Capoeira is like karate, but it is performed to music.

Brazil has one of the world's best football teams. Brazilians love to watch their team play.

Here, Brazil is playing against Chile. The Brazilians are in the yellow shirts.

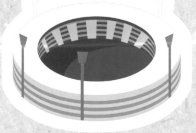

You don't have to go to a stadium to see a football match. Wherever you go in Brazil, you will see people playing football!

29

Make it yourself

Brazilians wear amazing masks at carnival time. Why not make your own colourful mask, then dress up and hold a carnival with your friends!

You will need:

- stiff card
- paper
- pencil
- scissors
- felt-tip pens
- glue
- glitter
- elastic tape

Step 1.

Draw a mask shape on your paper and cut it out. Check that your paper mask fits your face.

Your mask should be about this size and shape.

Step 2.

Trace the outline of your paper mask onto your piece of card. Decorate your card using felt-tip pens, glitter, or anything else you like.

You might like to add some feathers.

Step 3.

Use the points of your scissors to make a small hole at the two outer edges of the mask. Thread elastic tape through the holes and secure the tape with knots.

Now your carnival mask is ready to wear!

Useful words

ancestors   Family members who lived a long time ago.

carnival   A huge public party. Carnivals often celebrate an important day for the followers of a religion.

cog railway   A railway that runs up and down a very steep slope. Cog railways have trains with special wheels that fit into cogs on the railway track.

continent   One of seven large areas of land on the Earth. The seven continents are Africa, Antarctica, Asia, Australia, North America and South America.

hammock   A piece of strong cloth that is hung up by both ends and used as a bed.

settle   To travel to a different country and make a home there.

skyscraper   A very tall building with many floors. stilts wooden legs that support a house.

snorkelling   Swimming underwater with a mask and tube and a pair of flippers.

stilts   Wooden legs that support a house.

tropical   Hot and rainy.